WONDERFUL
WORLD OF
ANIMALS

For a free color catalog describing Gareth Stevens' list of high-quality books and multimedia programs, call 1-800-542-2595 (USA) or 1-800-461-9120 (Canada). Gareth Stevens Publishing's Fax: (414) 225-0377.
See our catalog, too, on the World Wide Web: http://gsinc.com

Library of Congress Cataloging-in-Publication Data

MacLeod, Beatrice.
    Amphibians / text by Beatrice MacLeod ; illustrated by Antonella Pastorelli.
      p. cm. -- (Wonderful world of animals)
    Includes bibliographical references (p. 31) and index.
    Summary: Introduces the physical characteristics, behavior, and habitat of various amphibians.
    ISBN 0-8368-1953-5 (lib. bdg.)
    1. Amphibians--Juvenile literature. [1. Amphibians.] I. Pastorelli, Antonella, ill.
II. Title. III. Series: MacLeod, Beatrice. Wonderful world of animals.
QL644.2.M313 1997
597.8--dc21   97-19506

This North American edition first published in 1997 by
Gareth Stevens Publishing
1555 North RiverCenter Drive, Suite 201
Milwaukee, Wisconsin 53212 USA

This U.S. edition © 1997 by Gareth Stevens, Inc. Created and produced with original © 1996 by McRae Books Srl, Via dei Rustici, 5 - Florence, Italy. Additional end matter © 1997 by Gareth Stevens, Inc.

Text: Beatrice MacLeod
Design: Marco Nardi
Illustrations: Antonella Pastorelli
U.S. Editor: Patricia Lantier-Sampon
Editorial assistants: Diane Laska, Rita Reitci

Note: Beatrice MacLeod has a Bachelor of Science degree in Biology. She works as a freelance journalist for Italian nature magazines and also writes children's nonfiction books on nature.

1 2 3 4 5 6 7 8 9 01 00 99 98 97

WONDERFUL WORLD OF ANIMALS

AMPHIBIANS

Text by Beatrice MacLeod
Illustrated by Antonella Pastorelli

Gareth Stevens Publishing
MILWAUKEE

WHAT IS AN AMPHIBIAN?

Amphibians vary enormously in size and shape. For example, some amphibians have long tails while others have none at all; some have four legs, some have two, and others have no legs. Unlike other vertebrates, which have hair, feathers, or scales to protect their bodies, amphibians have bare skin. They are divided into three groups.

4

Amphibians in the **Urodela** group have tails. This group includes newts, salamanders, and sirens.

Fire salamander

The second, and largest, group of amphibians is composed of frogs and toads. The group is called **Anura**, which means "without tails." Adult frogs and toads do not have tails.

Green toad

Caecilian

The third group is called **Gymnophiona** and is made up of caecilians. They have no legs and look like earthworms.

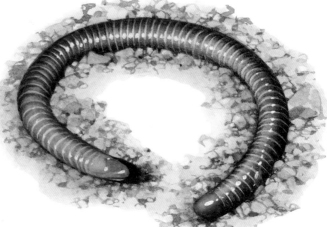

BORN IN WATER

The word *amphibian* comes from two ancient Greek words — *amphi* ("both") and *bios* ("life"). A typical amphibian spends its youth (larval stages) in water and its adult life on land.

1. Frogs, for example, lay their eggs in water. The soft eggs are protected by a jelly-like coating.

2. After about one week, the embryos develop heads and tails.

3. When tadpoles hatch, they have external gills and can swim using their tails. They have no legs (these develop later).

4. After a few weeks (or months, or even years in some species), the tadpole is completely transformed. The adult frog has no gills or tail. It has lungs and breathes directly from the air.

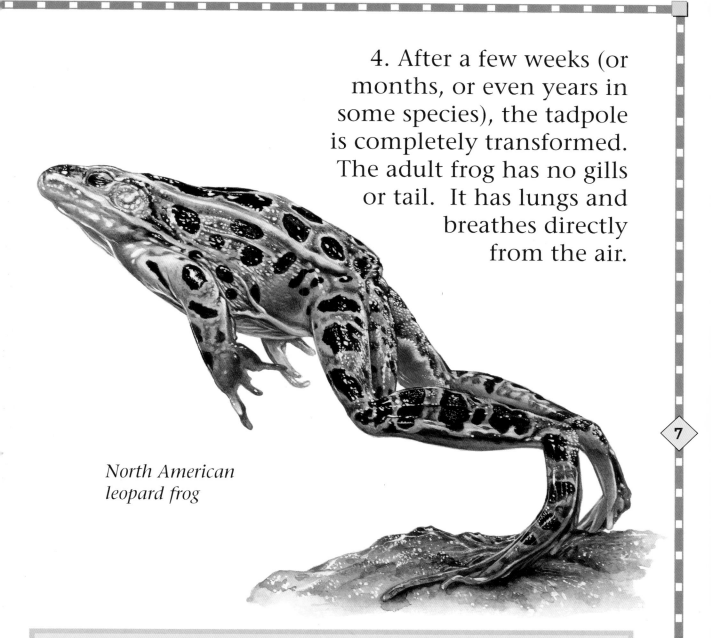

North American leopard frog

Amphibians in the story of evolution
Life began in the water about 4.5 billion years ago. Over millions of years, fish developed. Amphibians, the first animals able to breathe air and live on land, evolved from fish. In turn, amphibians eventually gave rise to reptiles, birds, and mammals.

LAND OR WATER?

Not all amphibians grow up in water and spend their adult lives on land. Many species of salamanders, for example, live and breed entirely on land. Some other amphibians spend all their lives in water.

Salamanders that reproduce on land lay their eggs in damp places, such as in rotting tree trunks. The larval stage occurs inside the egg, and the salamander is formed before it hatches.

Salamander's egg

When the egg breaks, a tiny salamander appears. It keeps its tail, but the gills disappear after a time. In some species, the gills remain in adulthood.

Young tiger salamander

Most **newts** spend spring and summer in water. They lay their eggs in spring and then build up reserves of fat to spend winter on land.

Red-spotted newt

FROGS AND TOADS

Most frogs and toads live in tropical and subtropical regions. A few species also live in other environments, such as deserts, mountains, grasslands, forests, and cities. They live on every continent except Antarctica.

Toads live in damp, dark places, often far from water. They are active mainly at night, or dusk and dawn, when they hunt for insects and small animals. Most species return to the water to breed.

Common toad

Surinam toad

The **Surinam toad**
spends its entire life in water.
During reproduction, the male toad
presses the fertilized eggs onto the female's
back. A protective skin grows over the eggs.
After about eighty days, the young hatch
as fully-formed miniature toads.

Frog or toad?
Most frogs have smooth, mucus-covered skins and long,
powerful back legs. They move by jumping and live in or
near water. Almost all toads have squat bodies, short legs,
and dry, rough skins. Less active than frogs, toads often
move on land by walking.

SALAMANDERS AND NEWTS

Salamanders and newts live in cool, temperate regions. Only one group of salamanders lives in the tropical zones of Central and South America. They live in a variety of habitats. Aquatic species live in rivers, lakes, and swamps. Land-dwellers live under rocks and logs. Some species burrow into the soil.

The North American **many-ribbed salamander** is one of several species of lungless salamanders. They breathe through their skin and the lining of their mouths.

Many-ribbed salamander

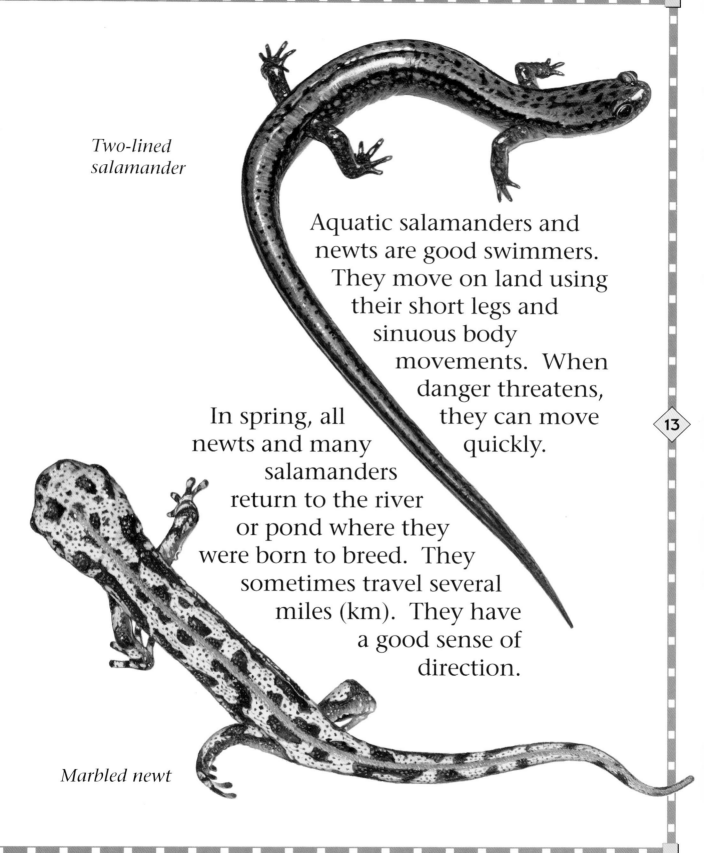

Two-lined salamander

Aquatic salamanders and newts are good swimmers. They move on land using their short legs and sinuous body movements. When danger threatens, they can move quickly.

In spring, all newts and many salamanders return to the river or pond where they were born to breed. They sometimes travel several miles (km). They have a good sense of direction.

Marbled newt

GETTING AROUND

Amphibians develop tails, legs, and organs in sizes that best serve their needs in nature. For example, an olm's streamlined body and long tail is ideal for swimming, whereas the toad's well-developed hind legs are useful for swimming and essential for leaping.

The **olm**, a blind salamander, lives in underwater caves in southeastern Europe. It has bright red gills, a long pale body, and tiny limbs.

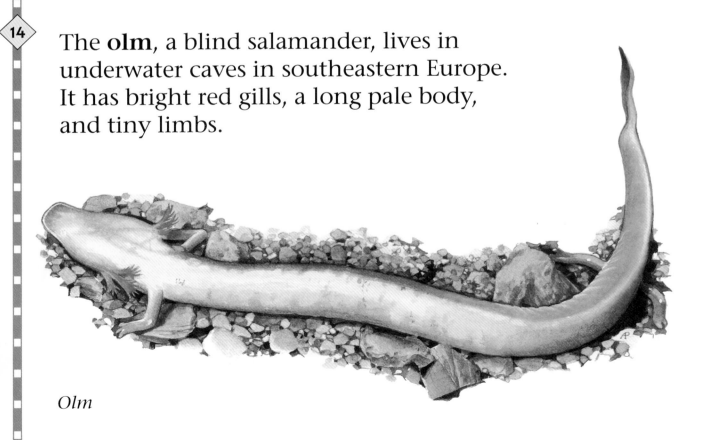

Olm

The **tree toad** has sticky spots on its fingers that help it cling to and move over smooth or slippery surfaces. Its powerful back legs allow it to make long leaps to escape predators or to surprise an insect or small animal.

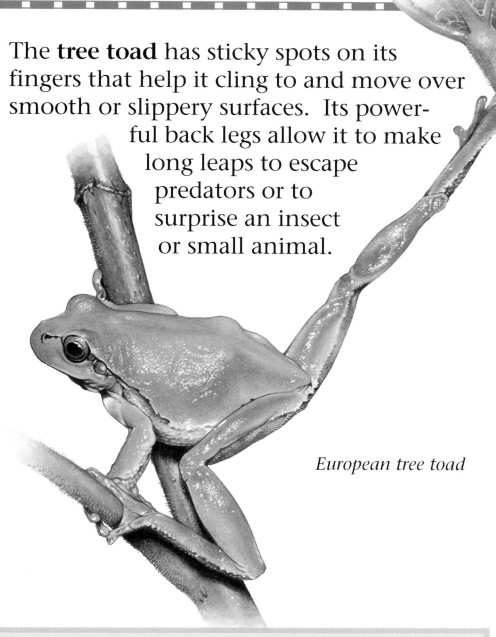

European tree toad

Cold-blooded animals
To maintain a constant body temperature, mammals and birds (warm-blooded animals) must eat regularly. Amphibians (cold-blooded animals) are able to adapt their body temperature to the surrounding environment. They use less energy and need less food.

WATER IS LIFE

Amphibians have soft, unprotected skins. They live in moist places to avoid drying out. On land, they stay under damp debris or near water. Some species, like the garden toad, stay in burrows during the day and only come out at night when there is more moisture.

Male crested newt

The **crested newt** of Europe and Asia grows to about 8 inches (20 centimeters) long and has a rough, warty skin. It gets its name from the crest that appears along the male's back and head during courtship. The male, slightly smaller than the female, does a very elaborate courtship dance.

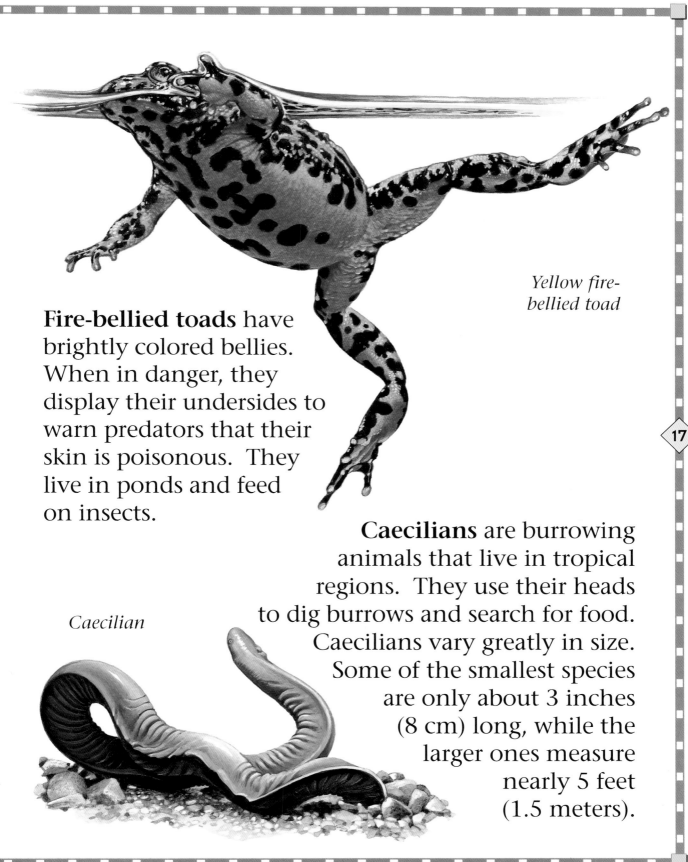

Yellow fire-bellied toad

Fire-bellied toads have brightly colored bellies. When in danger, they display their undersides to warn predators that their skin is poisonous. They live in ponds and feed on insects.

Caecilian

Caecilians are burrowing animals that live in tropical regions. They use their heads to dig burrows and search for food. Caecilians vary greatly in size. Some of the smallest species are only about 3 inches (8 cm) long, while the larger ones measure nearly 5 feet (1.5 meters).

FOOD

Amphibians eat other animals, including worms, spiders, termites, and insects of all sorts. In fact, some species will eat almost anything they can capture — even fish, reptiles, and mammals.

Japanese giant salamander

The **Japanese giant salamander** measures up to 5 feet (1.5 m) in length. It lives in mountain streams.

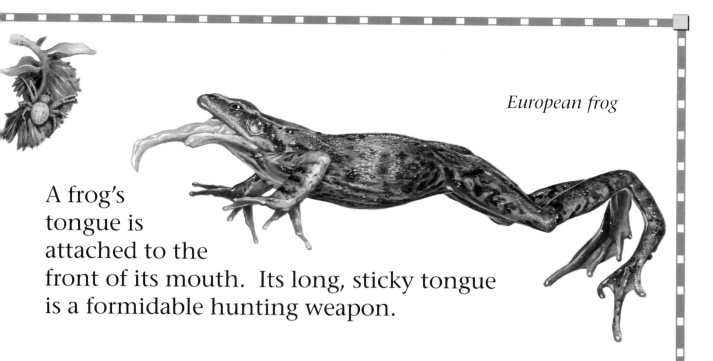

European frog

A frog's tongue is attached to the front of its mouth. Its long, sticky tongue is a formidable hunting weapon.

The bullfrog and the **South American horned frog** are among the fiercest amphibians. With their huge mouths, horned frogs can swallow a mouse whole!

South American horned frog

FANCY COLORS

Many amphibians are brightly colored with vividly patterned or marked skins. The colors are produced by three skin pigments — brown, yellow, and white. Some amphibians can change color. Amphibians use skin color for camouflage, to hunt without being seen, to warn predators they are poisonous, and to recognize others of the same species.

Darwin's frog

Tiny **Darwin's frog** conceals itself from predators with its dark green skin, which blends in with surrounding leaves. The male frog keeps its eggs and young in its vocal pouch until they can look after themselves.

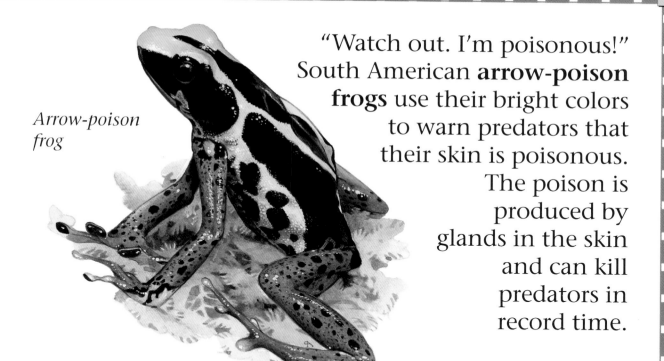

Arrow-poison frog

"Watch out. I'm poisonous!" South American **arrow-poison frogs** use their bright colors to warn predators that their skin is poisonous. The poison is produced by glands in the skin and can kill predators in record time.

Many animals keep safe by pretending to be more dangerous than they really are. Some harmless amphibians look like poisonous species, thus scaring off predators. Salamanders and newts have special glands on their skins that give off repulsive odors.

Salamander

METAMORPHOSIS

Metamorphosis is the term used to describe the dramatic changes amphibians undergo as they pass from the aquatic larval stage to adulthood. The process can last from just a few days to several years, depending on the species. Some amphibians keep juvenile features even as adults.

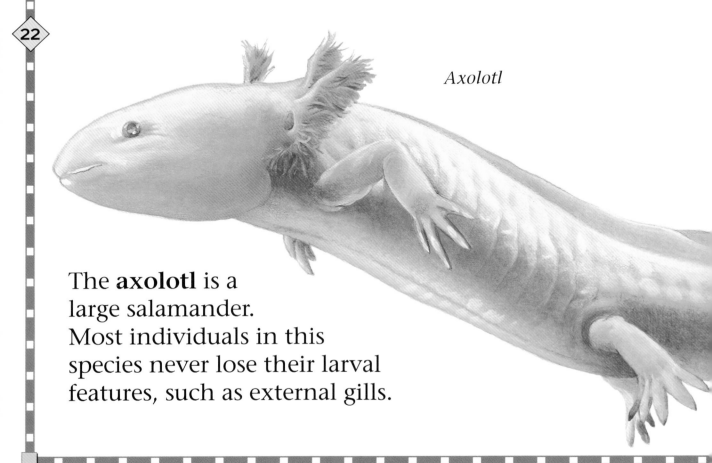

Axolotl

The **axolotl** is a large salamander. Most individuals in this species never lose their larval features, such as external gills.

The **rain frog** lives in the hot, tropical rain forests of Central and South America. Baby frogs develop inside a large, clear egg without ever becoming tadpoles or undergoing metamorphosis.

Amphibian records

The 0.5-inch (12-millimeter) **Cuban frog** is the smallest amphibian known; the **Japanese giant salamander** is the largest. An adult weighs about 55 pounds (25 kilograms) and may reach 5 feet (1.5 m) in length.

Above: A South American rain frog develops inside an egg.

PARENTAL CARE

Most amphibians lay eggs. Some females lay their eggs in water and leave them to hatch and take care of themselves as they grow. Other amphibian parents dedicate a lot of time to caring for their offspring.

After the female **midwife toad** lays her eggs (strings of about 40-50 eggs), the male attaches them to his hind legs. He keeps them safe and moist for about three weeks until they hatch as tadpoles.

Male midwife toad

A female pygmy marsupial frog in a bromeliad. Note the pouch with eggs on her back.

The female **pygmy marsupial frog** keeps her eggs in a pouch on her back until they hatch. She then deposits the tadpoles into water-filled bromeliads. Each week she returns to the bromeliads and lays a small clutch of unfertilized eggs on which the tadpoles feed until they turn into frogs.

Frog and toad eggs

Depending on the species, frogs and toads lay anywhere between five and several thousand eggs in water, on land, in trees, or on the male's or female's body. Laid together in blobs or long strings, the eggs are wrapped in a jelly-like substance or a protective foam.

FROG CHORUS

Male frogs and toads make a variety of calls, each with its own special meaning. They call to attract females, discourage rivals, and to recognize others of the same species. Sometimes thousands of frogs call together, making a frogs' chorus.

Rush frog

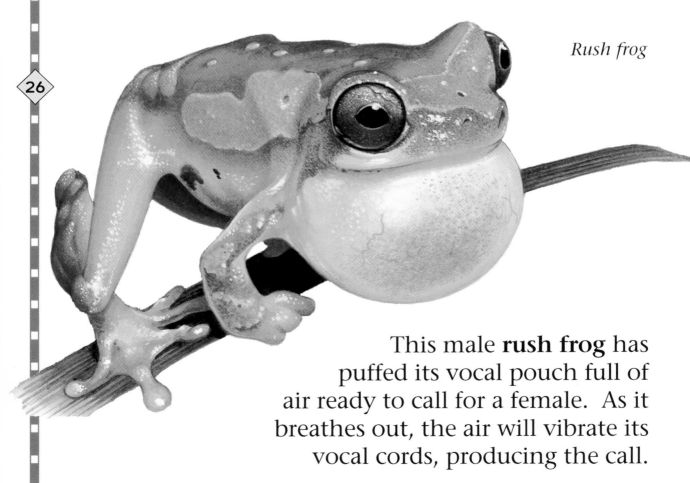

This male **rush frog** has puffed its vocal pouch full of air ready to call for a female. As it breathes out, the air will vibrate its vocal cords, producing the call.

Tungara frog

When the male **tungara frog** puffs out its vocal pouch to call for a mate, it makes itself an easy target for predators. Because of this, male tungara frogs stay together in groups when calling. This works to confuse the predators.

Types of calls

Each species of frog or toad has its own special call. These range from croaks and clicks to buzzing or humming to shrill whistles and trills. The length of the call can last from just a few milliseconds to several minutes.

GLOSSARY

adapt: to make changes or adjustments in order to survive in a changing environment.

aquatic: of or relating to water; living or growing in water.

breed (v): to join (animals) together for the purpose of producing young; to mate.

bromeliads: tropical American plants of the pineapple family, living either on the forest floor or on trees and rocks.

camouflage (n): the shape or color pattern an animal has that helps it blend into its surroundings, making it harder for predators to see.

courtship: the act of seeking the affections or approval of a prospective mate.

embryo: an animal in the very earliest stages of growth, usually in an egg after it has been fertilized.

environment: the surroundings in which plants, animals, and other organisms live.

evolve: to change or develop gradually from one shape or form to another. Over time, all living things must evolve to survive in their changing environments, or they may become extinct.

fertilize: adding male sex cells to the female egg to start the growth and development of a new individual.

gills: the breathing organs in all fish and some marine invertebrates. Amphibians at some stage have external gills.

glands: organs in the body that make and release substances such as sweat, tears, saliva, and poison.

habitat: the natural home of a plant or animal.

larval stage: in the life cycle of insects, fish, amphibians, and some other organisms, the stage that comes after the egg but before adulthood.

mucus: a slippery secretion that protects some cell layers.

pigment: a substance in plants or animals that gives them color.

predators: animals that kill and eat other animals.

reproduce: to produce young or offspring.

sinuous: wavy or snakelike.

species: animals or plants that are closely related and often similar in behavior and appearance. Members of the same species are capable of breeding together.

tadpoles: newly-hatched frogs or toads that live in water and have a tail and gills.

temperate zone: the regions between the tropics north to the Arctic Circle and south to the Antarctic Circle. These regions typically have mild temperatures and moderate humidity.

transform: to change in form or appearance.

tropical: belonging to the tropics, or the region centered on the equator and lying between the Tropic of Cancer (23.5 degrees north of the equator) and the Tropic of Capricorn (23.5 degrees south of the equator). This region is typically very hot and humid.

ACTIVITIES

1. Locate a small pond or stream where frogs live. In the spring, with the help of a grown-up, collect some frog spawn or tadpoles in a jar of the pond water and take them home. Keep the jar in a cool place. Spawn does not need to be fed and will hatch after some time. Tadpoles can be fed small amounts of leafy vegetation. Pond weed would be good. You can also feed them crumbled, hard-cooked egg yolk. Watch the tadpoles develop gills, then legs. Be sure to take them back to their pond when you have finished studying them.

2. Invite a toad to live in your garden. Toads eat the insects that can harm garden plants. Find four flat stones to make a toad house. Prop up three stones on edge for the sides and back. Place the fourth flat stone over them for a roof. Small spaces at the edges let in air. Find a round stone big enough to partly block the door. Fill a jar lid with water. Now carefully catch a toad for your garden. Put it in its new home, place the jar lid close to the open front, and block the rest of the space with the round stone. Every day, move the round stone a little bit to one side and add fresh water to the lid. After four or five days, your toad will stay in the garden by itself, happily eating insects. Be sure it always has fresh water.

3. Get for your own, or borrow, a pet frog, toad, or salamander. Prepare a home for it in a fish bowl or a small aquarium. Find out how to care for it. You can make a simple chart that will help you remember when to feed your pet and change its water.

Books and Videos

Amazing Frogs and Toads. Barry Clarke (Knopf)

Amphibians. (AIMS Media video)

Amphibians: What, When and Where. (International Film Bureau)

The Fascinating World of Toads. Angels Julivert and Carlos De Miguel (Forest House)

Frogs: An Investigation. (Phoenix/BFA Films and Video)

Frogs: Living in Two Worlds. Secrets of the Animal World series. Andreu Llamas (Gareth Stevens)

Frogs and Toads. (Wood Knapp Video)

Frogs, Toads, Lizards and Salamanders. Nancy W. Parker and Joan R. Wright (Morrow)

Red-Spotted Newt. Doris Gove (Simon and Schuster)

Reptiles and Amphibians (2 vols). Catherine H. Howell (National Geographic)

Salamanders. Emery Bernhard (Holiday House)

Salamanders. Ed Maruska (Child's World)

Snakes, Salamanders, and Lizards. D. Burns (NorthWord)

Toad Overload: A True Tale of Nature Knocked Off Balance in Australia. Patricia Seibert (Millbrook Press)

Web Sites

cgee.hamline.edu/frogs

frog.simplenet.com/froggy (*See* Scientific Amphibian)

INDEX